SCOTLAND
WORLD ADVENTURES

BY HARRIET BRUNDLE

BookLife
PUBLISHING

©2023
BookLife Publishing Ltd.
King's Lynn, Norfolk
PE30 4LS, UK

ISBN: 978-1-80155-955-3

All rights reserved.
Printed in Poland.

Written by:
Harriet Bundle

Edited by:
Charlie Ogden

Designed by:
Natalie Carr

A catalogue record for this book is available from the British Library.

All facts, statistics, web addresses and URLs in this book were verified as valid and accurate at time of writing. No responsibility for any changes to external websites or references can be accepted by either the author or publisher.

SCOTLAND
WORLD ADVENTURES

CONTENTS

Page 4	Where Is Scotland?
Page 6	Weather and Landscape
Page 8	Clothing
Page 10	Religion
Page 12	Food
Page 14	At School
Page 16	At Home
Page 18	Families
Page 20	Sport
Page 22	Fun Facts
Page 24	Glossary and Index

Words that look like **this** can be found in the glossary on page 24.

WHERE IS SCOTLAND?

Scotland is a country in the United Kingdom. The United Kingdom is in **Europe** and is made up of Scotland, Wales, England and Northern Ireland.

SCOTLAND

NORTHERN IRELAND

ENGLAND

WALES

The **population** of Scotland is over five million. The main language spoken in Scotland is English.

THE SCOTTISH FLAG

The capital city of Scotland is Edinburgh.

WEATHER AND LANDSCAPE

The weather in Scotland changes with the **seasons**. If is often warm in summer and cold in winter.

Scotland has many different **landscapes**. There are mountains, rivers and beaches in the country.

This is the Quiraing on the Isle of Skye.

CLOTHING

People in Scotland usually wear comfortable clothing. In the winter months there is often snow, so people wear coats and hats to keep warm.

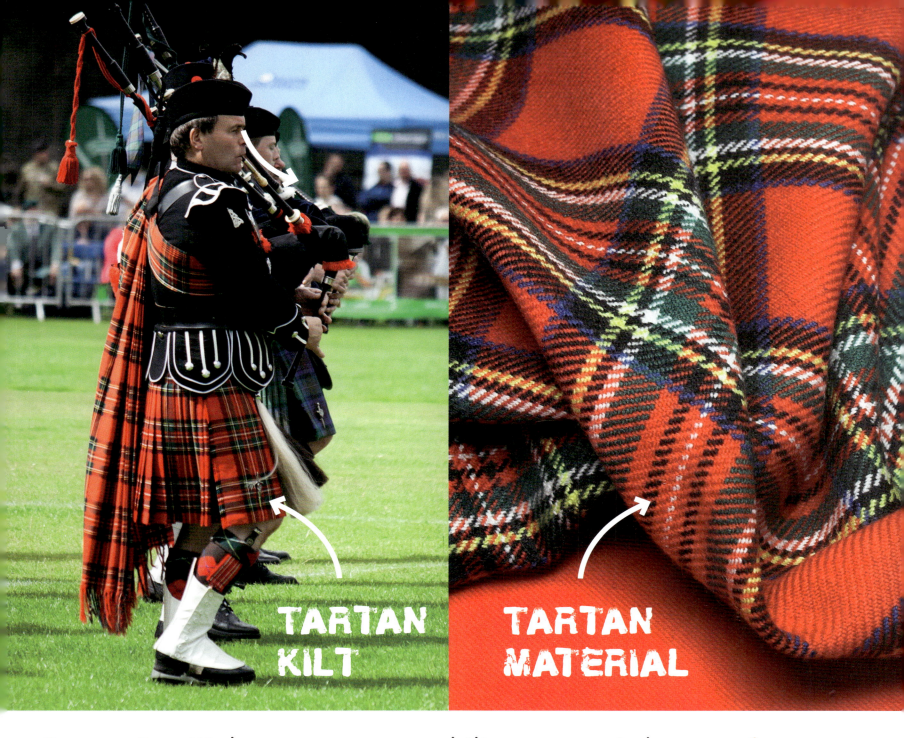

TARTAN KILT

TARTAN MATERIAL

Some Scottish men wear a kilt on special **occasions**, such as weddings. A kilt looks like a skirt. It is often made out of tartan material.

RELIGION

THIS CHURCH IS IN KEITH, SCOTLAND.

The **religion** with the most followers in Scotland is Christianity. A Christian place of **worship** is called a church.

Other people in Scotland follow different religions, such as Islam and Hinduism. Many people also choose not to follow any religion.

FOOD

HAGGIS

Haggis is a very popular food in Scotland. Haggis is made using **offal**, onions, spices and salt. It is boiled before it is eaten.

Cullen skink is a **traditional** Scottish dish. It is a thick soup that is made from fish, potatoes and onions.

CULLEN SKINK

AT SCHOOL

Children in Scotland start going to school when they are 4 years old. They usually leave school when they are 18 years old.

Some children in Scotland enjoy going to after-school clubs where they can play sports or learn how to play an **instrument**.

AT HOME

Some people in Scotland live in busy cities. In cities, there are tall blocks of flats and lots of restaurants and shops.

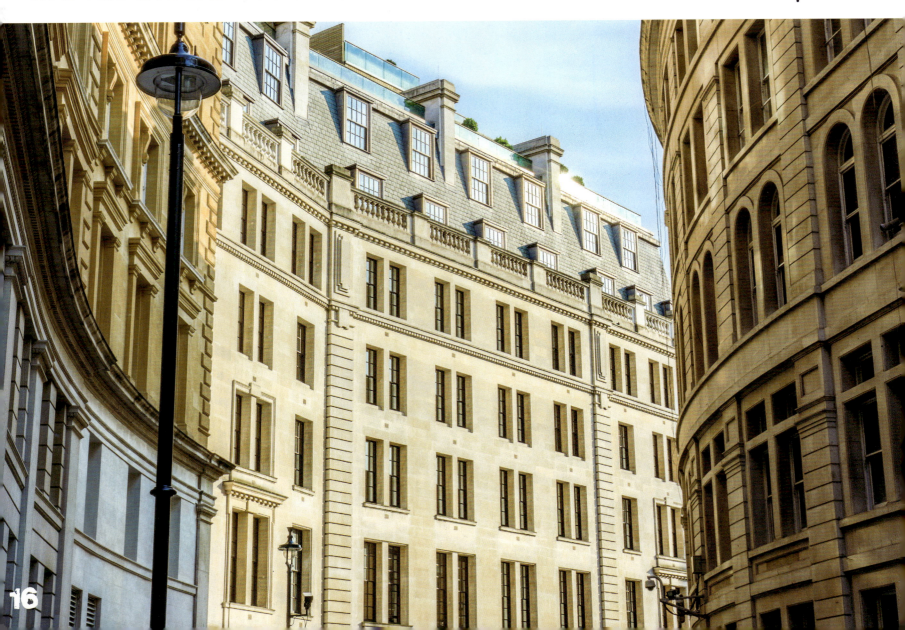

In the countryside, most people live in houses with gardens. There are lots of fields in the Scottish countryside.

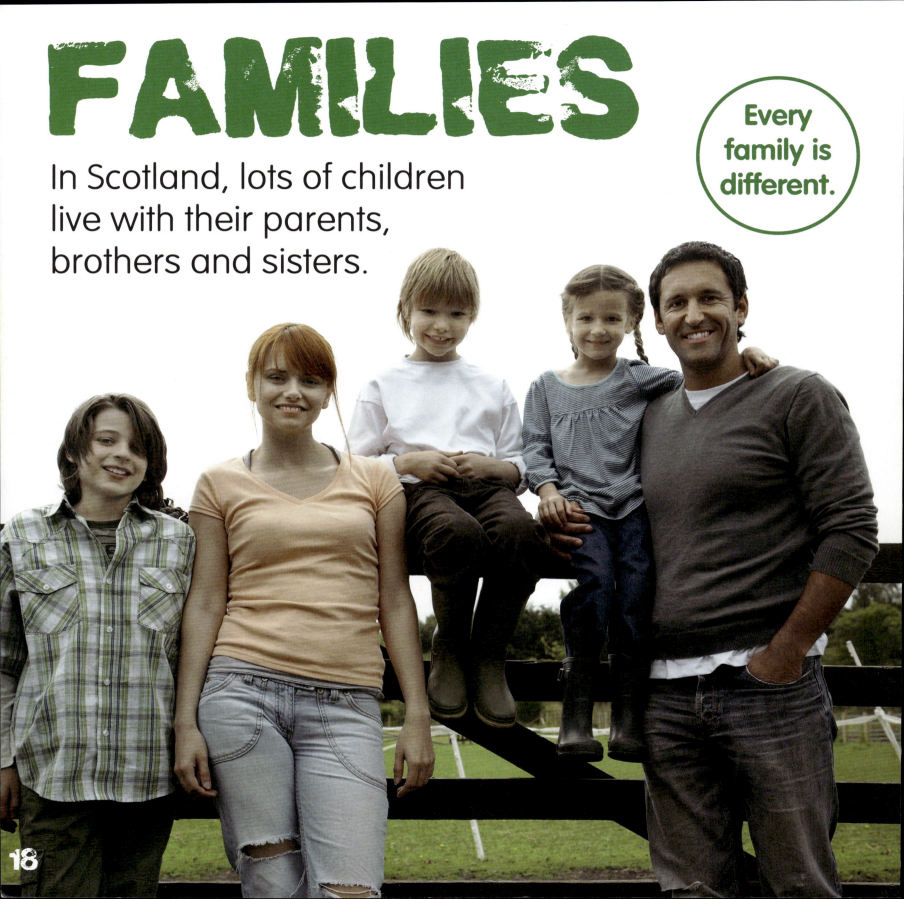

FAMILIES

In Scotland, lots of children live with their parents, brothers and sisters.

Every family is different.

Families often get together to celebrate special occasions, such as birthdays.

Children often get presents on their birthday!

SPORT

A popular sport in Scotland is football. Rangers and Celtic are two of the most popular football teams in Scotland. Both of these teams come from the city of Glasgow.

Golf is also very popular in Scotland. The game of golf was first played in Scotland!

FUN FACTS

Lots of different animals live in Scotland, including golden eagles and mountain hares.

MOUNTAIN HARE

GOLDEN EAGLE

BAGPIPE

The bagpipe is a traditional Scottish musical instrument. When someone squeezes air out of the pipes, the bagpipe makes a noise.

GLOSSARY

Europe   a large area of land that is made up of many countries, including the United Kingdom

instrument   an object that is played to make music

landscapes   everything that can be seen in an area of land

occasions   special events to celebrate

offal   the parts inside of an animal that can be used for food

population   number of people living in a place

religion   the belief in and worship of a god or gods

seasons   the four periods of the year: spring, summer, autumn and winter

traditional   related to practices or beliefs that have been around for a long time

worship   a religious act such as praying

INDEX

animals 22
children 14–15, 18–19
Christianity 10
cities 5, 16, 20
countryside 17
family 18–19
food 12
football 20
instruments 15, 23
school 14–15
seasons 6

Photo Credits:
Front Cover – Blaj Gabriel. 5 – Billy Stock. 6 – Heartland Arts. 7 – Kanuman. 8 – Tomsickova Tatyana. 9l – johnbraid. 9r – NemesisINC. 10 – Gail Johnson. 11 – ZouZou. 12 – bonchan. 13 – Fanfo. 14 – ESB Professional. 15 – SpeedKingz. 16 – I Wei Huang. 17 – grafxart. 18 – bikeriderlondon. 19 – Pressmaster. 20 – Herbert Kratky. 21 – Olimpik. 22 – withGod, FloridaStock. 23 – Gorosi. Images are courtesy of Shutterstock.com, unless stated otherwise. With thanks to Getty Images, Thinkstock Photo and iStockphoto.